Dedicated to my darling mummy X

A Date with Plantain

51 ideas & easy to cook fusion recipes

Patti Gyapomaa Sloley

Emmalily

Also by Patti and available on Amazon:

A Plate in the Sun: Modern Fusion Recipes from Ghana, Food from the African Soul

Ghana's Adinkra: Symbols from our African Heritage

Join Patti on:
www.pattismenu.com
www.facebook.com/pattismenu
@PattiSloley

A date with Plantain

Foreword

Patti has once again out-done herself in her new book and provided the readers with such a fabulous explanation of how to incorporate readily available products in Europe into her wonderful style of flavour filled cooking.

Having known Patti for several years and valued her huge contribution to my Novelli Academy in Hertfordshire not only for corporate and individual events but also as a resident Chef in the Academy offering her own unique expression and passion for food, I know that you, your family and friends will enjoy using this inspiring recipe book.

This book not only explains successfully the health benefits of plantain but also its underestimated versatility that Patti has managed to explain in such an easy to follow method.

Bon appetit.

Jean-Christophe Novelli

Michelin and 5AA Rosette
Award winning French chef

jeanchristophenovelli.com

I have always considered cooking as a form of art, after all you start with loads of ingredients of various textures, colours, smell and taste and you mix them together to create your work of art…. the plate is the frame, the cook the artist; so if you run with my idea the dishes that he /she creates will have to reflect the mood, origins and passion of the person cooking.

Patti has managed to capture all of this in her book, and if you have never had the pleasure of meeting Patti in person you have only got to read through the book and cook some of the recipes to understand the kind of person she is.

I first met Patti on my first visit to the Novelli Academy some 3 years ago, and I have had the pleasure to work with her on a regular basis since. We often discuss the similarity between Italian and Ghanaian cuisine, the dishes her mother and grandmother prepared and how easy it is nowadays to find the same ingredients used back home in Ghana.

 True to her Ghanaian origins, Patti cooks from the heart but she is not afraid to break the traditions of family dishes and make them hers by adding new ingredients here and there. In A Date with Plantain Patti takes a basic staple ingredient and creates an array of interesting, fun dishes packed full of exploding flavours.

Even traditional dishes have received the "Plantain Patti" makeover, go on give plantain a go!

Felice Tocchini

Chef and owner of Fusion Brasserie and Fusion Too

fusionbrasserie.com

Patti is one of those bubbly chefs that bring out the best in everyone. Her knowledge is amazing, especially when combining the best of Ghanaian, African and British dishes. On her courses at the Novelli Academy Patti clearly enjoys sharing recipes that are fun, easy and work every time.

Everyone loves her cooking techniques and the way she presents her food with vibrancy and colour. It is clear that her mum is also a great cook and has passed on many wonderful family recipes we can all enjoy.

Trish Davies

Food stylist, home economist and writer

trishdavies@aol.com

The enthusiasm, zest and vigour of Patti never ceases to amaze me. Often when I have the good fortune to see her at the Novelli Academy, where we sometimes conduct cooking classes, she's ready, willing and able to offer new ideas and tips on wholesome recipes with a few simple ingredients.

Ghanaian cuisine is not dissimilar to Indian dishes and the spices are the key to many of the recipes and their flavours. I love how pepper, nutmeg, ginger and onions are the comfort zone ingredients that Indian and Ghanaian cuisine share. Plantains are also popular in India and Patti manages to combine the flavours of ingredients and spices effortlessly to create simple yet delicious dishes.

Her passion for plantain shines through every part of the book. My personal favourite is Galliano, Plantain and Passionfruit Griddle. It's an easy to prepare dessert that can be made in minutes. Totally awesome! As you go through the recipes, there's no doubt that you'll be spoilt for choice in picking dishes to cook time and time again whatever the occasion.

Manju Malhi.

Chef, food consultant and writer

manjumalhi.com

If anyone could take up the daunting task of creating 51 tantalizing ways to cook with a single ingredient, it would have to be my fabulously creative and daring sister Patti.

Patti has always been a natural: her sense of dress style; her flair for cooking; her memorable meals; an artist in every sense of the word; the perfect hostess. Spend five minutes with her and her effect lingers.

Patti maintains an extraordinary balance between creativity and conformity and her ability to step out of the norm defines her. She always brings something different and her natural artistry comes across in her vibrant dishes. Hers is food from and for the soul.

I remember getting teased by my friends at Cardiff University for constantly quoting her on the importance of eating healthily.... "According to your sister" was my name for that entire semester!

So go ahead and explore Patti's dishes. She's been guided from the start by our mum, who constantly reminded us of the importance of good cooking and eating well, because " edziban gyengen, ni dzi yeyaw", to wit " lousy food is hard to eat!".

David Ampofo

Patti's brother, talk-show host, Managing Director, Channel Two Communications

www.channeltwo.co

Introduction

If you don't know how easy it is to cook delicious dishes with plantain you may be in for a pleasant surprise. It's easy to find, quick to cook, nutritious and delicious. These 51 ways with plantain have something for everyone - smoothies, snacks, starters, salads, mains, desserts and tapas-style entertaining tips.

Why focus on plantain I hear you ask. I had so many positive comments about the plantain recipes in A Plate in the Sun that I planned a plantain chapter for my next book. Once I started talking through ideas with friends I quickly realised that this chapter *was* my next book. There's nothing complicated about cooking with plantain and I'm sure you will find it enjoyable. Is it the perfect ingredient?

One of the many exciting things about plantain is its versatility and ability to combine with other tastes and textures. Its distinct and subtle flavours across all stages of ripeness, from green to yellow to black, can bring variation and another layer to favourite recipes. I sometimes break with tradition and explore classic recipes to create fusions from around the world. From burgers to brownies, to chutneys to dim sums. From a simple grilled snack like "Kofi-Brokeman", to a Sunday special of plantain stuffed lamb, there's a lot to discover and enjoy - little wonder plantain is so popular across more than half the planet including Africa, the Caribbean, Asia and the Americas.

Writing this book has been an absolute pleasure and I hope it inspires you to try something different and have fun in your kitchen. You may fall in love with it and begin a life-long affair.

Peel it, dice it, spice it, fry it!

Steam it, poach it, bake it, grill it!

Welcome to A Date with Plantain.

Finding, choosing, peeling, using

Finding

Plantain has been around in Afro-Caribbean and Asian food shops for just about as long as the shops have been there and has become so popular that more and more supermarket chains now stock it in the fresh produce section.

It takes about 8 days to go from green to yellow and about another 8 days from yellow to black. So, if you can't find black ones, buy yellow ones and wait….

Choosing

Plantain starts life green and unripe, firm and starchy. As they ripen the skins turn yellow and the flesh softens as the starch starts to convert to sugar. They continue their journey to full ripeness with the skins going a mottled black and then full black, the flesh goes soft and mushy and becomes sweeter and aromatic. Avoid buying shrivelled, squashy or mouldy ones.

Peeling

You can't peel a plantain like you would a banana as the skins are just too tough, so you need a knife.

The simplest way is to cut off and discard the plantain ends. Slice in half crossways and then lengthways.

If you want to keep the flesh in one piece, cut off the ends and run the tip of the knife in a single cut along the full length, just into the flesh, then peel the skin sideways, a bit like taking off a coat.

With green plantain the skin is really tough so you may need to make several full length cuts and peel it in sections.

To avoid staining your hands with the starch from green plantain you may want to wear gloves or peel under running water.

Using

Green - a good alternative to potato, perfect for crisps, canapés and mashes. To boil, cut them lengthways and again crossways, cook for about 20-25 minutes and then peel the skin when cooled.

Yellow & yellow-**black** - at its most versatile and an interesting change or compliment to many vegetables. Using yellow, just going black or yellow-black is a matter of personal taste. The more black markings the softer and sweeter the flesh will be.

Steaming time varies with the thickness of the pieces and stage of ripeness and normally takes about 5-8 minutes for ripe plantain. The flesh colour will change from a pale peach to yellow as it cooks.

Black - at its sweetest and an excellent ingredient for sweet and savoury dishes. Like bananas, store plantain at room temperature and out of sunlight, not in the fridge. They can be peeled and the flesh frozen until you are ready to use it.

Plantain on its journey from chips to puddings

Savoury

Some of these recipes are my take on timeless classics. Kelewele for example is an early evening treat and very popular in Ghana's colourful and lively night markets. You can't miss its tantalizing aroma wafting through the tropical night breezes …. just follow your nose…

Other recipes are more contemporary and simply how I like to enjoy plantain in my day to day cooking.

Picture - Herby fried plantain

Kofi Brokeman gets a makeover

snack, dessert

Borodze totoe is probably one of the cheapest street foods in Ghana and very nutritious. It is simply ripe plantain grilled and served with peanuts. Affectionately called Kofi Brokeman, because when you are down on your luck and broke the ubiquitous plantain seller is a welcome sight. Shaded by her sombrero, and patiently turning plantain over hot coals, you know she will chase away your hunger. I like to grill it with honey and sesame seeds.

Serves 2

2 plantains - ripe - yellow skin
honey to drizzle
sesame seeds to sprinkle

1. Cut off and discard the plantain ends. Slice in half crossways and then lengthways. Discard the skin.

2. Score the rounded sides of the plantain in a criss-cross pattern, being careful not to cut all the way through, drizzle with honey and sprinkle with sesame seeds.

3. Place on an oiled baking tray, scored side up and grill for about 8 minutes, until caramelised and golden.

Serve warm.

Plain grilled plantain spread with peanut butter has to be one of the quickest snacks ever

Grilled plantain also appears in A Plate in the Sun - no plantain cookbook would be complete without it!

Tip - try a sprinkle of cinnamon sugar before grilling

Oto
starter

If you are looking for a simple plantain mash this is it, real comfort food. **Oto** Is a traditional Ghanaian dish, made with yam by the Fantis (my mum) and plantain by the Ashantis (my dad) and both versions are great. It is served in small portions as a taster to kick start special occasions, like birthdays, coming of age, anniversaries and weddings. Although my Grandma Gyapomaa never waited for special occasions and rustled one up on every visit.

1 plantain - just ripe - skin just turned yellow
1 onion, diced
¼ scotch bonnet chilli, de-seeded
3 tbsp peanut butter
2 tbsp palm fruit oil
peanuts or cashews to serve

1. Cut off and discard the plantain ends. Slice in half crossways and then lengthways. Discard the skin. Steam for 5-8 minutes, place in a mixing bowl, mash until smooth and set aside to cool.

2. Pulse the onion and chilli in a blender then mix with the peanut butter, palm fruit oil and the mashed plantain. You may find warming the peanut butter for a few seconds in the microwave makes it easier to use.

Serve in a shallow bowl and scatter with nuts.

I like to garnish Oto with boiled eggs and avocado

Tip - for a simple mash just use plantain and peanut butter

Kelewele
snack or starter

Traditionally **kelewele** is diced, spiced and fried plantain. I prefer mine oven baked.

Serves 4

2 plantains - ripe - yellow skin just
starting to turn black
1 tbsp grated ginger
chilli flakes to taste
2 tsp zha'atar
1 tsp cumin seeds
salt and pepper to season
½ tsp cinnamon
½ tsp nutmeg, grated

Preheat oven to 180°C/fan 160°C/350°F/gas 4

1. Peel the plantain, dice then divide the pieces equally between 4 bowls.

2. Add the ginger and chilli flakes to one bowl, zha'atar to another and cumin to a third. Season these 3 bowls with salt and pepper.

3. Add the cinnamon and nutmeg to the fourth bowl.

4. Toss each bowl individually to coat the plantain with the spices.

5. Line a baking tray with foil and scrunch the foil to make 4 separate compartments to keep the flavours separate.

6. Tip the plantain into the individual compartments and bake for 20-25 minutes until golden and caramelised.

Sweetcorn Tatale

snack and main

Tatale is a classic Ghanaian savoury pancake, normally fried on a large black iron skillet. Call me biased, but my Grandma Elizabeth made the best tatale ever and for me the taste and aroma is a comforting childhood memory.

I like to add sweetcorn for the texture and taste, grated courgette works equally well.

Serves 2

2 plantains - over-ripe - black skin
¼ scotch bonnet chilli
1 onion, roughly chopped
1cm/½ inch fresh root ginger,
peeled and grated
140g/5oz plain flour
salt to season
1 spring onion, finely sliced
100g/3½oz sweetcorn, pre-cooked

oil to shallow fry

1. Peel the plantain and place in a blender together with the other ingredients, except the sweetcorn and oil, and whizz to form a batter. Stir in the sweetcorn.

2. Heat a large frying pan, add a little oil then pour half cups of batter in to form individual pancakes. Fry over a moderate heat until bubbles appear.

3. Turn the pancakes over and continue to fry until cooked through, pressing and flattening the pancake with a palette knife as it cooks.

4. Transfer to absorbent kitchen paper and keep warm whilst you cook the rest.

Serve on their own as a snack, or with a bean stew.

Tip - you can use ground rice
instead of flour

Crispies
snack and garnish

Simply crisps

Plantain crisps are eaten all over Africa and similar to potato crisps. Although you can buy them in packets I often like to make my own. Eating them just-cooled is an experience you can't find in a packet.

2 plantains - unripe - green skin

oil to shallow fry

Tip - I love them as a scoop for ceviche and hummus, or crushed and sprinkled on desserts, curries and salads

1. Peel then slice the plantain into thin discs with a sharp knife or mandolin.

2. Soak in cold water for about 10 minutes to remove excess starch. Drain, rinse and dry with kitchen paper.

3. Lower the pieces carefully into hot oil and fry until golden. Move them around in the pan to prevent them sticking to each other.

4. Remove from the oil, drain on kitchen paper, allow to just cool and serve.

If you prefer to oven bake rather than fry spread them out on a baking tray and bake for about 15-20 minutes 170°C/fan 150°C/340°F/gas 3

Chilli cheddar snack

1 plantain - ripe - skin just turning yellow
6 tbsp grated cheddar
½ tsp chilli flakes

Tip - try desiccated coconut instead of the cheese and chilli flakes

Preheat oven to 200°C/fan 180°C/390°F/gas 6

1. Peel then slice the plantain into discs about 5mm (¼ inch) thick.

2. Spread on a lightly oiled baking tray and bake in a preheated oven for about 20 minutes.

3. Remove the tray from the oven and sprinkle the cheese then the chilli flakes over each plantain disc. Return to the oven and bake until the cheese is just melted.

4. Remove from the oven and leave to cool slightly before serving.

Best eaten warm.

Herby fried plantain
main, snack, side dish

Frying is probably the most popular way of cooking plantain in Africa, Asia, the Caribbean and the Americas, seriously simple and seriously good. I like wedges of plantain with parsley, sage, rosemary and thyme.

In Ghana it's sometimes peeled then deep fried whole and often called *lolochi*

Serves 2-4

2 plantains - ripe - yellow skin
small handful of fresh mixed herbs,torn
2 garlic cloves, crushed
salt and pepper to season

oil to shallow fry

1. Peel then cut the plantain into chunky pieces - horizontal slices, diagonal discs or whichever way takes your fancy.

2. Mix the plantain with the remaining ingredients, except the oil.

2. Lower carefully into hot oil and fry for about 5 minutes, until they turn yellowy with crispy brown edges.

3. Drain and place on kitchen paper before serving.

Plantain and beans is another classic dish and commonly called Red-Red in Ghana. Both are typically cooked in palm fruit oil which gives the dish its distinctive taste and reddish colour

Tip - for a light lunch serve with mango and avocado salsa or baked beans

Stuffed lamb breast

main

Lamb is *just* my favourite - chops, breasts, leg, shoulder. Here I pair it with a plantain stuffing.

Serves 4

Stuffing:
3 shallots, finely chopped
1 plantain - ripe - yellow skin
50g/2oz shitake mushrooms, chopped
2 garlic cloves, minced
2 tsp fresh sage, chopped
50g/2oz Sweet corn
1 tsp freshly grated ginger
4 tbsp fresh breadcrumbs
½ tsp cumin seeds, optional
salt and pepper to season

1kg/2lb lamb breast, de-boned

oil to shallow fry

Preheat oven to 160°C/fan 140°C/325°F/gas 3

1. Sauté the shallots until translucent and set aside.

2. Peel and mash the plantain then mix in the shallots and remaining stuffing ingredients.

3. Lay the lamb breast flat, cut away any excess fat and season on both sides with salt and pepper. Cut into pieces roughly 15cm (6 inch) square and create pockets by gently prising the layers of meat apart, being sure to leave 3 sides attached.

4. Fill the pockets with the stuffing and secure with cocktail sticks.

5. Place the stuffed pieces on a roasting rack, cover with foil and roast for 2 ½ hours. Remove the foil after 1 hour.

Serve with vegetables and gravy or rice and a spicy sauce.

Tip - if you want to feed several people ask your butcher to bone a full leg of lamb. Then stuff, tie with string to hold it together and adjust the cooking time

Green plantain canapé - Tostones

snack

These are great party nibbles. Serve these canapé bases with tasty toppings like hummus, guacamole, olives and, my absolute favourite, ceviche.

Serves about 6-8

3 plantains - unripe - green skin
salt and pepper to season

oil to shallow fry

1. Heat the oil in a frying pan.

2. Peel the plantain and slice into 10 mm (½ inch) thick discs.

3. Carefully lower the plantain into the hot oil and fry until tender, usually about 2 minutes on each side.

4. Remove from the oil and drain on kitchen paper.

5. Gently flatten each piece to about 5 mm (¼ inch) using a rolling pin then return to the pan and fry for about 2 minutes on each side until golden and crispy.

6. Remove from the oil, drain on kitchen paper and season.

Add the toppings and serve.

Meatloaf

main

As an AFS exchange student in America, it made my day to come home from school and find my American host mum, Ethel Barker, had made meatloaf for dinner. Here I have added a kick with chillies and an interesting sweetness with plantain.

Serves 4

2 medium onions, finely chopped
2 garlic cloves, minced
225g/8oz minced beef
225g/8oz minced lamb
225g/8oz Sausage meat
1 tbsp tomato puree
1 tbsp Worcester Sauce
1 tsp dried mixed herbs
salt and pepper to season
2 green chillies, chopped
14 rashers smoked streaky bacon
1 plantain - ripe - yellow skin

oil to shallow fry

Preheat oven to 200°C/fan 180°C/390°F/gas 6.

1. Sauté the onions and garlic until soft and translucent. Remove from the heat, put into a mixing bowl and leave to cool.

2. Add the remaining ingredients, except the bacon and plantain, and mix.

3. Line a loaf tin cross ways with the strips of bacon and add half the meat mix.

4. Peel the plantain and lay it whole along the length of the tin, then spoon in the remaining meat. Wrap the bacon ends over the top of the loaf and cover with foil.

5. Bake for 30 minutes, remove the foil, drain off any oil and bake for a further 30 minutes. Insert a skewer into the centre and if it comes out clean your meat loaf is ready.

6. Pour off any fat and leave to cool slightly.

Enjoy it hot or cold.

35

Spicy relish

side dish

Here's a quick, vibrant and flavoursome relish for meat, fish and any vegetables you have to hand.

Serves 2-4

1 plantain - just ripe - skin just turned yellow
1 tsp chilli flakes
1 chopped onion
2 garlic cloves, minced
1cm/½ inch ginger, cut into fine strips
250g/9oz cherry tomatoes
1 scotch bonnet chilli, de-seeded and minced
1 tsp tomato puree
1 orange bell pepper, de-seeded and chopped
1 tbsp Worcester Sauce
salt and pepper to season

oil to shallow fry

Preheat oven to 180°C/fan 160°C/350°F/gas 4

1. Peel then chop the plantain into chunks, and season with the chilli flakes. Bake for 20-25 minutes on a lightly oiled baking tray.

2. Whilst the plantain is baking use a large sauté pan to fry the onions, garlic and ginger until the onions are lightly golden.

3. Add the remaining ingredients to the pan and stir. Leave to cook for 10 -15 minutes. Add the plantain and toss before serving.

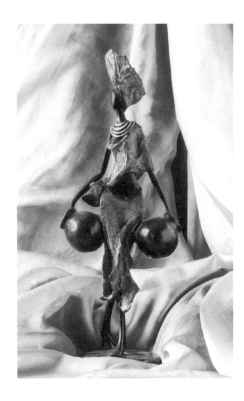

Stem ginger & plantain chutney
side dish

1 tbsp mustard seeds
100g/3½oz onions, finely chopped
1 scotch bonnet chilli, de-seeded
and chopped
½ tsp grains of paradise, optional
1 plantain - ripe - yellow-black skin
50g/2oz dates, stoned and
chopped
50g/2oz dried figs, chopped
115ml/4floz cider vinegar
230ml/8floz pineapple juice
100g/3½oz raisins
50g/2oz stem ginger, chopped
2 tsp curry powder
½ vanilla bean, split and scraped
or ½ tsp vanilla bean paste
pinch of salt

oil to shallow fry

1. Heat the oil in a pan and add the mustard seeds. Once the seeds start popping, add the onions, chilli and grains of paradise and fry for about 5 minutes, stirring frequently, until the onions are soft.

2. Peel and dice the plantain.

3. Add the plantain, dates and figs to the pan, stir, partially cover and simmer for about 10 minutes.

4. Add the remaining ingredients, bring to the boil and simmer for a further 20-25 minutes until the mixture thickens.

Spoon the chutney into a sterilised jar and leave to cool before sealing and refrigerating.

Serve with hot and cold meat dishes, on crackers or with your favourite cheese.

Lamb curry & Takoradi dumplings

main

Growing up in Takoradi, *Kakro* was my introduction to street food and I like to call them "Takoradi dumplings". This dish always fills the house with that irresistible aroma that has even the postman popping his head in the kitchen window to ask "Mmm, what's cooking?".

Serves 4

750g/24oz stewing lamb, chopped
1 tsp brown mustard seeds
2 red onions, sliced
2 garlic cloves, crushed
2cm/1 inch ginger, freshly grated
1 tsp turmeric
2 tsp curry powder
2 scotch bonnet chillies, pricked
1 cinnamon stick
1 tsp cumin seeds, lightly toasted
50g/2oz red lentils
1 tsp sugar
50g/2oz creamed coconut, grated
1 chicken stock cube
kaakro dumpling mix (page 51)

oil to shallow fry

Tip - I like to include lamb breast for its distinctive taste. Before adding to the curry at step (2) chop the breast into pieces and roast on a rack for 30-40 minutes to drain off excess fat 200°C/fan 180°C/390°F/gas 6

1. Heat the oil in a large saucepan and brown the lamb, remove and set aside. Using the same pan, lightly fry the mustard seeds. Once they start popping add the remaining ingredients, except the creamed coconut and stock cube. Fry until the onions are lightly golden.

2. Add the lamb and creamed coconut.

3. Dissolve the stock cube in 200 ml boiling water and add to the pan. Cover and leave to simmer for about 30 minutes. Add scoops of the Kaakro mix and continue to simmer until the lamb is tender and the Kaakro cooked through.

Serve with rice and steamed okra.

Salt fish & eggs in spicy tomato

main

This is one of those meals I prepare when I'm in a hurry and can't decide what to eat! I like to bulk cook tomato sauces and always have some ready. So for this recipe, it's just a case of adding salt fish and plantain to the sauce and dinner's ready in no time.

Serves 4

1 onion, thinly sliced
2 garlic cloves, crushed
1cm/½ inch ginger, peeled and
freshly grated
1 scotch bonnet chilli, chopped
2 tbsp prawn powder
2 tsp tomato puree
400g/14oz tin chopped tomato
dash Worcester Sauce
1 plantain - ripe - yellow skin
100g/3½oz salt-fish fillets, flaked
2 eggs, boiled, shelled, halved

oil to shallow fry

1. Heat the oil in a large sauté pan. Fry the onions, garlic, ginger and chilli until the onions are lightly golden.

2. Add the prawn powder, tomato puree, tomatoes and Worcester Sauce. Cook for 10 minutes.

3. Peel then cut the plantain flesh into 2cm/1 inch wedges.

4. Add the plantain, salt fish and boiled eggs to the pan with a splash of water, cover, bring to a simmer and cook for a further ten minutes.

Serve with chunks of soft boiled yam, rice or roast sweet potato and a scattering of torn basil or parsley.

Tip - salt-fish varies in its saltiness. To reduce the amount of salt soak in hot water for a few minutes before cooking. Smoked haddock is a good alternative

Plantain toad in the hole

main

A popular classic with a difference.

Serves 3-4

1 plantain - ripe - yellow skin
500g/16oz good quality sausages
1 onion, cut into wedges
1 tbsp rapeseed oil
150g/5oz plain flour
1 egg
300ml/11floz semi-skimmed milk
1 tsp sage, chopped
leaves from a sprig of thyme
½ tsp curry powder
¼ tsp turmeric
¼ tsp cumin seeds
2 garlic cloves, crushed
salt and pepper to season

Preheat oven to 220°C/fan 200°C/430°F/gas 7.

1. Peel and cut the plantain into 2cm/1 inch chunks and place them together with the sausages and onion wedges in an oven-proof baking dish.

2. Drizzle with the oil and roast for 15 minutes until everything starts to brown.

3. Whilst the sausages are roasting, put the flour in a bowl and whisk in the egg and milk to form a smooth batter.

4. Stir in the remaining ingredients and put in the fridge.

5. Once the sausages are ready, pour in the batter.

6. Cook for another 25-30 minutes until crispy and golden.

Tip - serve with gravy and a
steamed green vegetable

Plantain in blankets

side dish, party nibble

A simple breakfast, a light lunch with a salad or as part of a mixed grill supper.

Serves 4

2 plantains - ripe - yellow skin
8 sprigs of thyme
8 slices smoked streaky bacon

Preheat oven to 200°C/fan 180°C/390°F/gas 6

1. Cut off and discard the plantain ends. Slice in half crossways and then lengthways. Discard the skin.

2. Strip the leaves from the thyme and discard the stalks.

3. Sprinkle the thyme leaves on the plantain then wrap each piece with a rasher of bacon.

4. Place on a rack on a baking tray and roast until the bacon is crisp and golden, about 15 minutes.

Tip - for party style nibbles cut each cooked piece into 3 and serve on cocktail sticks

Green mango salad & spicy plantain croutons

starter, side dish

My friend Agnes introduced me to this delicious green mango salad, popular in parts of French-speaking Africa. Here I partner it with plantain for a simple and refreshing starter. Sweet and sour African style?

Serves 4

2 unripe green mangoes (green skin and hard to the touch)
2 garlic cloves, minced
2 tbsp rapeseed oil
juice of 1 lime
salt and freshly ground black pepper to season

1. Peel the mango, slice, cut into thin strips and place in a bowl.

2. Mix the remaining ingredients and pour over the mango, stir to combine.

3. Cover with cling film and refrigerate for an hour.

For plantain croutons follow the Kelewele recipe (page 23).

Serve the croutons hot with the chilled salad, garnish with flat leaf parsley and sprinkle with chilli flakes.

As a side dish it changes simple roast chicken to something special

Tip - the mango needs to be hard when squeezed, if it gives it's too ripe

Apitsi or Kaakro?

side dish, snack, savoury dessert

Apitsi is a sweet and savoury pudding and *Kaakro* a deep fried dumpling, both made from exactly the same ingredients yet given completely different personalities depending on how they are cooked - mouthfuls of pleasure either way.

2 plantains - over-ripe - black skin
¼ scotch bonnet chilli,
de-seeded if you wish
2cm/1 inch ginger, peeled, freshly grated
1 onion, chopped
120g/4oz plain flour
salt to season

1. Peel the plantain then put the flesh in a blender with the chilli, ginger and onion, roughly blend then tip into a bowl.

2. Mix in the flour and salt.

3. Follow the instructions for Apitsi or Kaakro below.

Apitsi

In Ghana we love a slice of this dense, savoury plantain pudding as a snack with peanuts. I find it is also a winner with beef as an alternative to Yorkshire puddings and a pleasant change to stuffing to accompany roast pork

Preheat oven to 200°C/fan 180°C/390°F/gas 6

Stir 3 tablespoons of rapeseed oil into the mix then spoon into a greased baking tin. Bake in a preheated oven for about 40 minutes, until a skewer inserted into the middle comes out clean

Ofam is one of many variations and uses palm oil in the mix. We also call it *Bodoo-ngo.*
(Picture right)

Tip - cornmeal or ground rice works as an alternative to flour

Tip - For a rustic look bake in aromatic pandan leaves which can be found in Chinese and Thai supermarkets. Bruise the leaves to release the aroma

Kaakro

These deep fried plantain dumplings are a popular street snack in Ghana. Simply form the mix into egg-size dumplings and deep fry or, for soft dumplings, drop scoops into stews and curries and simmer until cooked through (page 41)

Aranitas

snack or garnish

Puerto Rican friends in America introduced me to this crunchy snack which gets its name from the Spanish for little spiders. Believe me, it's much nicer than its name suggests.

Serves 2

1 plantain - unripe - green skin
2 tsp garlic powder
½ tsp cayenne pepper
salt and freshly ground pepper to
season

oil to shallow fry

1. Peel the plantain and coarsely grate the flesh into a bowl.

2. Add the remaining ingredients and mix.

3. Carefully place heaped tablespoonfuls into the hot oil. Fry until crisp and golden, turning once.

4. Drain on kitchen paper.

Serve as a snack with cold drinks or as a garnish for salads.

Tip - dusting with cayenne pepper
adds extra bite

Plantain, prawn & pork dim sums

snack, starter or party nibble

I absolutely love Chinese dim sums and had to find a way of incorporating plantain. Delicious!

Dumpling filling:
½ plantain - ripe - yellow skin
100g/3½oz lean pork mince
10 tiger prawns, peeled, de-
veined, roughly chopped
½ scotch bonnet chilli, sliced and
de-seeded
1 tbsp freshly grated ginger
2 garlic cloves, minced
1 banana shallot, finely chopped
1 tbsp light soy sauce
2 tsp sesame oil
2 tsp corn flour
salt and pepper to season

To wrap:
12 wonton wrappers
1 egg, beaten

1. Cut off and discard the plantain ends. Slice in half crossways and then lengthways. Discard the skin. Steam for 5-8 minutes, mash then leave to cool.

2. Put the plantain and remaining dumpling filling ingredients into a bowl and mix.

3. For each dumpling, brush the surface of a wonton wrapper with egg wash then place 2 teaspoons of the filling in the middle. Bring the sides of the wrapper together and shape into a ball leaving the top open.

4. Place the dumplings in an oiled bamboo steamer, making sure they don't touch each other. Cover and place over a pan of boiling water. Steam for 8-10 minutes until the dumplings are cooked through and firm when squeezed.

Serve with a sweet chilli dipping sauce or something fiery, like Shitor (a Ghanaian shrimpy relish) mixed with soy sauce.

Tip - shitor is available in afro-Caribbean food shops, markets and some supermarkets

Creamed spinach & plantain

side dish

Stewed spinach served with boiled plantain is another classic Ghanaian combination. Here's a quick and simple twist, an easy side dish for a quick lunch or supper and perfect company for grilled fish.

Serves 2

1 plantain - ripe - yellow skin
200g/7oz baby spinach
3 shallots, peeled, chopped
sliver of scotch bonnet chilli, chopped
salt and pepper to season

oil to drizzle

1. Cut off and discard the plantain ends. Slice in half crossways and then lengthways. Discard the skin. Steam with the spinach for 5-8 minutes.

2. Coarsely blend the spinach, shallots and chilli.

3. Add the plantain and seasoning and pulse briefly to combine.

Pour into a bowl, drizzle with the oil and serve.

Patti Gyapomaa Sloley

Caramelised sweet potato & plantain

side dish, snack or party nibble

Here's something different to enjoy with drinks on a warm summer evening.

Serves 2

1 plantain - ripe - yellow skin
225g/8oz orange sweet potatoes
2 tbsp rapeseed oil
black pepper to season
2 tbsp honey
juice of 1 lemon
pinch of sesame seeds

Preheat oven to 200°C/fan 180°C/390°F/gas 6.

1. Peel the plantain, cut into diagonal pieces and place in a bowl.

2. Cut the sweet potato into wedges, add to the plantain, drizzle with the rapeseed oil, season and mix.

3. Tip onto a baking tray and roast in the oven for 20-25 minutes until golden.

4. Mix the honey and lemon juice, pour over the sweet potatoes and plantain and return them to the oven for 5 minutes or a little longer if you prefer more crunch.

Remove from the oven and serve scattered with sesame seeds.

Salmon nicoise

starter, main

Traditionally this salad often includes tomatoes, tuna, eggs, potato, greens beans and olives. Here I use salmon and plantain instead of tuna and potato.

Serves 4

1 plantain - ripe - yellow skin
115g/4oz green beans

Marinade
2 garlic cloves, minced
zest and juice of 1 lime
1 tbsp honey
sliver of scotch bonnet chilli, chopped
salt and pepper to season
drizzle of sesame oil

3 salmon fillets
2 plum tomatoes, quartered
1 spring onion, sliced diagonally
4 anchovy fillets
olives, green and black, to scatter
2 tbsp capers

Dressing:
small handful of basil
small handful of mint
1 tbsp rapeseed oil
juice of ½ lemon
salt and pepper to season

2 boiled eggs, quartered to garnish

Serve garnished with the eggs

1. Peel and chop the plantain and steam with the green beans for 5-8 minutes, then set aside to cool.

2. Mix the marinade ingredients in a bowl, add the salmon and coat. Leave to marinate for at least 15 minutes.

3. Grill the salmon until cooked through, remove from the grill and set aside to cool.

4. In a large bowl combine the tomatoes, spring onions, anchovies, olives, capers, beans and plantain. Flake the fish and add.

5. Blend the dressing ingredients and drizzle over the salad.

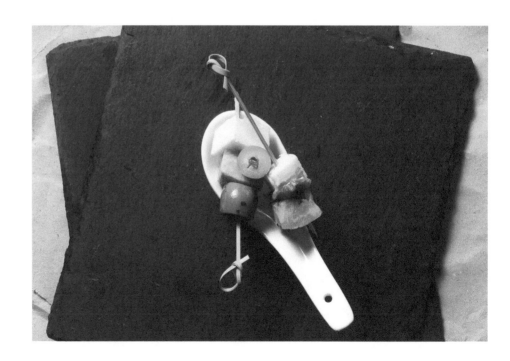

Plantain gnocchi
main

Gnocchi is one of those comfort foods that works well with many different base ingredients. My friend, and top Italian chef Felice, regularly delights guests at the Novelli Academy with mouth-watering variations like sweet potato and beetroot. Here plantain is the base ingredient.

Serves 2-4

2 plantains - ripe - yellow skin
100g/3½oz plain flour
25g/1oz parmesan cheese, grated
1 egg yolk
salt and pepper to season
nutmeg, freshly grated to taste

1. Cut off and discard the plantain ends. Slice in half crossways and then lengthways. Discard the skin. Steam for 5-8 minutes then mash and leave to cool.

2. Add the remaining ingredients, mix together then knead to form a soft dough.

3. Bring a large pan of salted water to the boil.

4. On a floured surface roll the dough into a sausage shape about 1.5 cm (½ inch) diameter.

5. Cut into pieces about 1.5cm (½ inch) long and toss in flour to prevent sticking. Roll each piece over the prongs of a fork to make indents to hold the sauce.

6. Line a tray with a clean napkin, dust with flour and transfer the gnocchi pieces to it.

7. Carefully tip the gnocchi into the boiling water and cook for about 3 minutes. Once the pieces float they are cooked.

8. Use a slotted spoon to remove the gnocchi from the water and place in a bowl.

I like to serve with a spicy tomato sauce and shavings of parmesan.

Bangers & Mash - plantain, carrot & apple

main

An interesting take on a British classic dish that also goes well with pork roasts and grills.

Serves 2

4 good quality sausages
2 carrots, sliced
1 plantain - ripe - yellow skin
¼ tsp vanilla bean paste, optional
1 tbsp grainy mustard
4 tbsp apple sauce
salt and freshly ground black
pepper to season

1. Cook the sausages in your favourite way.

2. Whilst the sausages are cooking steam the carrots for about 15 minutes, until just soft.

3. Cut off and discard the plantain ends. Slice in half crossways and then lengthways. Discard the skin. Steam for 5-8 minutes.

4. Put the carrots, plantain, vanilla, mustard, apple sauce and seasoning in a bowl and coarsely mash.

Serve with a gravy or sauce.

Tip - leftovers mixed with grated cheese and wrapped in shortcrust pastry makes a curious sweet-savoury veggie pie

If you would like to make your own apple sauce:

3 apples (like braeburn or cox), cored and peeled
2 tsp lemon juice
1 tsp sugar
2 tbsp water
½ tsp mixed spice or cinnamon
½ tsp nutmeg

Dice the apples and place in a pan with the other ingredients and a splash of water. Simmer until soft and mushy.

65

Chicken & quinoa one-pot
starter or main

This recipe is based on **Nkaakra**, or **light soup** and the plantain flavour works like potato - possibly the Ghanaian equivalent of Jewish chicken soup.

Serves 6-8

2kg/4lb chicken pieces, bone-in
salt to season
2cm/1 inch ginger, peeled
1 scotch bonnet chilli, pierced
1 stock cube
2 sprigs fresh thyme
400g/14oz tin tomatoes
4 garlic cloves, crushed
2 onions, roughly chopped
2 carrots, chopped
1.5l/54floz boiling water
1 plantain - just ripe - yellow skin
100g/3½oz quinoa

1. Put the chicken, salt, ginger, chilli, stock cube and thyme into a large saucepan.

2. Blend the tomatoes, garlic and onions until smooth, pour over the chicken then cover and simmer for about 20 minutes.

3. Add the carrots and water and simmer until the meat is just tender and cooked through, stirring occasionally. Taste and adjust the seasoning.

4. Peel the plantain and cut into bite size pieces.

5. Add the plantain and quinoa and leave to cook until the quinoa grains separate and the plantain is soft.

Add spinach, mushrooms or shallots for variety. Serve on its own or with steamed rice.

Spiced up pork & plantain burgers

main or as miniatures for party nibbles

I've used pork here, but lamb or beef is equally scrumptious.

Makes 4 big burgers

1 plantain - ripe - yellow skin
450g/16oz pork mince
1 red onion, finely chopped
2 tsp grated root ginger
sliver of scotch bonnet chilli,
chopped
3 garlic cloves, minced
2 tsp curry powder
4 tbsp fresh breadcrumbs
1 tsp dried mixed herbs
4 tbsp grated parmesan cheese
salt and pepper to season

1. Peel and mash the plantain, place in a bowl with the remaining ingredients and mix together.

2. Divide and shape into four burgers. Press your thumb into the centre of each burger to make an indent to help the burger remain flat and even-shaped as it cooks.

3. Heat a griddle pan, brush each burger with oil and griddle for about 4-5 minutes on each side, until completely cooked through.

Serve the burgers in soft bread rolls topped with a relish and a little grated cheddar. Thin slices of red onion and tomato with a lettuce leaf add crunch and colour.

Tip - I like to serve it with a soft, buttery avocado and sweetcorn salad for the creamy texture and taste

His & Hers sarnies

snack or main

One for the girls and one for the guys!

Serves 2 - or 1 hungry bricky

4 rashers smoked back bacon
1 plantain - ripe - yellow skin
2 soft bread rolls

oil to shallow fry

Builder's bacon butty

Short, simple, satisfying

1. Cut off and discard the plantain ends. Slice in half crossways and then lengthways. Discard the skin.

2. Fry the plantain in a lightly oiled pan for about 3 minutes each side, until soft.

3. As the plantain fries, grill the bacon until crisp.

Layer the rolls with the plantain and bacon. A few slices of jalapeño with a dollop of ketchup, or a spread of mustard, adds a little heat. A steaming mug of tea completes the picture.

Serves 2

2 rashers smoked streaky bacon
1 plantain - ripe - yellow skin
2 slices of well-seasoned roast chicken
shredded lettuce leaves
2 thin slices beef tomato
2 slices Swiss cheese

For the dressing:
3 tbsp mayonnaise
1 tsp ketchup
pinch of cayenne pepper
pinch of curry powder
pinch of garlic powder

Ladies light lunch

Less carbs than you may think – there's no bread here!

1. Grill the bacon until just crisp and set aside.

2. Cut off and discard the plantain ends. Slice in half crossways and then lengthways. Discard the skin.

3. Grill the plantain for 3 minutes on each side.

4. Remove from the grill, roll flat with a rolling pin and grill again for 2 minutes each side.

5. Mix the dressing ingredients whilst the plantain is grilling.

6. With the plantain still warm, assemble the sandwich with the bacon, remaining ingredients and dressing.

7. Secure with a cocktail stick and serve.

71

Rustic roast veggies with chorizo
side dish

A simple and smoky side dish to something meaty or fishy.

Serves 4

1 plantain - ripe - yellow skin
1 large sweet potato
1 courgette
3 banana shallots, peeled, halved
2 garlic cloves, crushed
1 dried bay leaf, crushed
2 sprigs rosemary
100g/3½oz chorizo sausage, chopped
drizzle of rapeseed oil

Preheat oven to 200°C/fan 180°C/390°F/gas 6.

1. Peel the plantain.

2. Cut the plantain, sweet potato and courgette into wedges and place in a bowl.

3. Add the remaining ingredients, drizzle with the oil and mix together.

4. Roast in a shallow oven proof dish for about 20 minutes until golden and serve.

Tip - for a vegetarian dish leave out the chorizo and sprinkle the vegetables with 2 teaspoons of smoked paprika before roasting

Prawn & plantain fritters

snack, starter, party nibble

Based on a delicious Filipino fritter, I use julienne strips of green plantain for the crunch. I can't stop my lips smacking as I wait for the prawns to turn pink.

Serves 4

8 tiger prawns, peeled, de-veined
and butterflied, tails left on
2 garlic cloves, minced
sliver of scotch bonnet chilli,
chopped
salt and pepper to season
2 tbsp corn flour
2 egg whites
1 plantain - unripe - green skin
1 spring onion, cut into thin strips

1. Mix the prawns with the garlic and chilli, season and set aside.

2. Whisk the corn flour and egg whites in a bowl to form a batter.

3. Peel the plantain and cut into thin strips using a julienne peeler. Discard the soft centre.

4. Add the plantain and onion to the batter and gently mix to coat.

5. Form fritters by encasing each prawn in the mix and pressing together, leaving the tails sticking out. Place on a tray and chill for 30 minutes to allow the batter to firm up.

6. Heat the oil in a sauté pan and gently fry the fritters for 2-3 minutes each side until golden brown and the prawns are cooked through.

7. Drain on kitchen paper and serve hot.

The salad bar

main, side dish

These salads start with a feast for the eyes – an easy way towards five-a-day!

1 plantain - ripe - yellow skin
100g/3½oz black beans
100g/3½oz baked beans
100g/3½oz black-eye beans
100g/3½oz chick peas
100g/3½oz sweet corn
1 onion, chopped
½ orange bell pepper, diced
1 tomato, de-seeded, diced

Dressing:
2 garlic cloves, minced
3 tbsp rapeseed oil
2 tbsp fresh lime juice
sliver of scotch bonnet chilli, finely chopped
½ tsp celery seasoning
salt to season
pinch of sugar

Beans & things

1. Cut off and discard the plantain ends. Slice in half crossways and then lengthways. Discard the skin. Steam for 5-8 minutes, leave to cool then dice.

2. Combine the remaining salad ingredients in a bowl and add the plantain.

3. Mix the dressing, pour over the salad and gently mix.

Serve garnished with fresh basil.

1 plantain - ripe - yellow skin
½ red onion, thinly sliced
2 garlic cloves, minced
sliver of scotch bonnet chilli
1 carrot, cut into julienne strips
2 tsp freshly squeezed lemon
1 tbsp honey
115ml/4floz hot stock or boiling water

oil to shallow fry

Warm spicy plantain

1. Peel then slice the plantain into 1cm (½ inch) rounds and fry for 3-4 minutes, turning once.

2. Stir in the onions, garlic, chilli and carrot and fry until the onions are lightly golden.

3. Stir in the lemon juice, honey and stock. Simmer until the liquid is syrupy.

Scatter with coriander leaves and crushed peanuts before serving.

Easy cheesy capers

A colourful salad of warm roast vegetables dressed in garlic and cumin.

1 plantain - ripe - yellow skin
100g/3½oz butternut squash
½ red bell pepper, de-seeded
½ yellow bell pepper,
de-seeded
1 tsp cumin seeds
1 tsp coriander seeds
pepper to season
drizzle of rapeseed oil for roasting
2 tbsp, rapeseed oil for dressing
1 tbsp cider vinegar
2 garlic cloves, minced
100g/3½oz feta cheese, crumbled
2 tbsp capers

Preheat oven to 200°C/fan 180°C/390°F/gas 6.

1. Peel and dice the plantain and squash and place in a bowl.

2. Dice the bell peppers and add to the bowl.

3. Mix in the cumin seeds, coriander seeds and season.

4. Tip onto a baking tray, drizzle with roasting rapeseed oil and roast in the oven for about 15-20 minutes, until cooked through.

5. Mix the dressing oil, vinegar and garlic in a bowl, add the cooked vegetables and gently mix.

6. Cover with cling film and stand for 10 minutes or until you are ready to serve.

Pour onto a platter and scatter with the cheese and capers.

Tip - for added colour I like to halve and de-seed a romano pepper, rub with oil and bake for about 20 minutes, then pile in the salad

Penang beef & plantain curry
main

You've probably got most of the dry ingredients in your kitchen cupboard already. Once you've assembled them and blended the sauce, the rest is simply a piece of cake... or curry.

Serves 4

700g/24oz braising beef, chopped
2 onions, chopped
2 tbsp tomato paste
2cm/1 inch ginger chopped
3 garlic cloves, crushed
1 tbsp soy sauce
2 tsp shrimp powder
2 tsp paprika
2 tsp cayenne/chilli powder
1 tsp ground coriander
1 tsp whole cumin seeds
2 green chillies, whole
1 scotch bonnet chilli, pricked
½ tsp turmeric
½ tsp cinnamon
pinch of nutmeg
½ tsp ground cloves
400ml/14floz coconut milk
juice of ½ a lime
1 plantain - ripe - yellow-black skin
3 tomatoes, quartered
salt to season

oil to shallow fry

Tip - try galangal as an alternative to ginger

1. Heat the oil in a large saucepan and brown the beef.

2. Place all the ingredients except the beef, plantain and tomatoes in a blender and blitz to form a paste.

3. Stir the paste into the meat, cover and leave to cook for 45 minutes to an hour or until the meat is reasonably tender, stirring occasionally.

4. Peel and chop the plantain and add to the curry. Add the tomatoes. Bring to the boil, then reduce to a simmer for a further 15-20 minutes until the meat is very tender and the plantain cooked through.

Serve with rice and scatter with torn basil. A sprinkle of crushed plantain crisps or crushed cashews adds an interesting crunch.

81

Crispy stuffing balls

side dish, snack

Plantain and almond stuffing balls. These can be enjoyed as an alternative to sage and onion stuffing.

100g/3½oz carrots
1 plantain - ripe - yellow skin
1 onion, chopped
3 garlic cloves, minced
3 tbsp rapeseed oil
25g/1oz stem ginger, sliced and chopped, optional
50g/2oz breadcrumbs
100g/3½oz hazelnuts, chopped
freshly grated zest of 1 orange
1 egg, beaten
salt and pepper to season

oil to shallow fry
oil to brush

Preheat oven to 200°C/fan 180°C/390°F/gas 6.

1. Slice the carrots, steam until just tender, then finely chop.

2. Whilst the carrots are steaming, cut off and discard the plantain ends. Slice in half crossways and then lengthways. Discard the skin, then steam for 5-8 minutes. Mash and leave to cool.

3. Heat a pan, add the oil and fry the onions and garlic until the onions are soft and translucent then put into a bowl to cool.

4. Add the remaining ingredients and plantain, season and mix together.

5. Using damp hands roll scoops of stuffing into truffle-size balls. Arrange them on a tray lined with parchment paper, brush with oil and bake for 20-25 minutes until golden.

Serve with roast meats.

Plantain cheese straws

snack

1 plantain - ripe - yellow skin
100g/3½oz cream cheese
pinch chilli flakes
1 tsp fresh sage, finely chopped
salt and black pepper to season
1 sheet puff pastry, shop bought
1 egg, beaten
1 tsp sesame seeds

Preheat oven to 200°C/fan 180°C/390°F/gas 6.

1. Cut off and discard the plantain ends. Slice in half crossways and then lengthways. Discard the skin. Steam for 5-8 minutes, then set aside to cool.

2. Mash with the cream cheese, chilli, sage and seasoning to form a smooth paste.

3. Place the puff pastry on a floured surface and brush all over with the egg. Using a palette knife spread the plantain mix evenly across the pastry surface and sprinkle the sesame seeds.

4. Fold in half and press gently to seal. Slice into 1 cm (½ inch) straws and twist the straws twice. Bake for about 20 minutes or until puffed and golden.

Cheese stuffed plantain

main, snack

My friend Amanda tells me this is a popular dish in her Columbian home and I can see why...

Brunch, lunch or supper - enjoy it any time!

Serves 4

4 plantains - ripe - yellow skin
4 thick slices of mozzarella cheese
4 tsp chopped jalapeño pepper

oil to brush

Preheat oven to 200°C/fan 180°C/390°F/gas 6.

1. Peel the plantain and place on a baking sheet. Brush with the oil and bake for 20 minutes until golden on both sides. Remove from the oven and make a slit along the top.

2. Stuff with the cheese and chopped jalapeño and serve as the cheese melts.

Tip - stuff it like you would put toppings on your favourite pizza. Perhaps: ham and cheese, mushrooms and cheese, baked beans and cheese, chilli con carne, stewed black eye beans, chorizo sausage, caramelised onions

Sweet things
Adoko-doko-dze

The plantain's natural sweetness in its latter stages of ripeness makes it a natural ingredient for sweet things, or "adoko-doko-dze" as Ghana's coastal Fanti people often call it.

It can often reduce the need for added sugar and in most of my dessert recipes I leave refined sugar out completely. It's just so easy to make a sweet treat from a ripe plantain.

Picture - Candied gooeys

Plantain chocolate brownies

This is a good excuse for coffee with a friend, or when you're ... hold it. Who needs an excuse to enjoy a brownie?

Serves 4-6

1 plantain - ripe - yellow-black skin
150g/5oz butter
200g/7oz dark chocolate
3 eggs
50g/2oz caster sugar
2 tsp vanilla extract
100g/3½oz plain flour
1 tsp coffee granules
50g/2oz pistachio nuts, shelled, crushed
25g/1oz walnuts, shelled, crushed

Preheat oven to 180°C/fan 160°C/350°F/gas 4

1. Line a 20 cm (8 inch) square tin with baking parchment.

2. Peel and mash the plantain.

3. Gently melt the butter and chocolate in a pan over a low heat, stir until melted, combined and smooth. Take care not to overheat or the chocolate will split.

4. Beat the eggs, sugar and vanilla extract together in a bowl, then mix in the melted chocolate.

5. Sift in the plain flour, add the coffee and fold until the mixture is glossy.

6. Tip into the lined tin and randomly drop heaped teaspoon-size blobs of the plantain onto the mix.

7. Scatter the nuts over the top. Drag a skewer or cocktail stick through the plantain to give a marbled effect.

8. Bake for 25 -30 minutes depending on how you like your brownie, more baking time makes the brownie centre less gooey. Allow to cool before cutting into squares.

Tip - adding freeze dried or frozen raspberries to the mix before pouring adds colour

Pear, raspberry & plantain pud

No eggs, no sugar, no butter, no kidding! Its sweetness comes from the natural sugars in the fruits. I first made this pudding with guava and now with pear and raspberry. It certainly works with a combination of just about any fruit – fresh, tinned, frozen, or dried.

Serves 6-8

2 plantains - overripe - black skin
½ tsp mixed spice
½ tsp grated nutmeg
100g/3½oz sultanas
100g/3½oz raspberries, fresh or frozen
1 tsp almond extract
400g/14oz tin pear halves, drained and chopped
2 tbsp rapeseed oil
150g/5oz plain flour
2 tsp baking powder

Preheat oven to 180°C/fan 160°C/350°F/gas 4

1. Peel and mash the plantain.

2. Add all of the ingredients except the flour and baking powder and gently mix.

3. Sieve in the flour and baking powder and gently mix.

4. Spoon into a greased tin and bake for 50 to 60 minutes or until a skewer inserted into the middle comes out clean.

Serve with mascarpone or ice cream.

Tip - decorate with a scattering of toasted almond flakes

93

Candied gooeys

It's fruity, it's spicy, it's gooey – what else do you need?

Serves 2

1 plantain - ripe - yellow skin
2 tbsp honey
115ml/4floz orange juice
pinch ground black pepper
1 tsp fresh ginger, grated
½ tsp cumin seeds
1 star anise
1 cinnamon stick

Preheat oven to 200°C/fan 180°C/390°F/gas 6.

1. Peel the plantain and chop into cylindrical chunks about 1cm (½ inch) thick and place in a baking dish.

2. Whisk the honey and orange juice together and stir in the remaining ingredients, then pour over the plantain chunks.

3. Bake for about 30 minutes until the glaze is syrupy and sticky and the plantain soft, basting every 10 minutes.

Before serving, spoon some of the syrupy glaze over the chunks. Great with ice cream.

Stuffed Medjool dates

Whole medjool dates with a cream-cheese and plantain stuffing, now this is just too easy to eat before your guests even arrive.

Serves 4

½ plantain - ripe - yellow skin
12 medjool dates
50g/2oz cream cheese

1. Cut off and discard the plantain ends. Slice in half crossways and then lengthways. Discard the skin. Steam for 5-8 minutes and allow to cool.

2. Slice the dates lengthways to make room for the filling. Be sure not to cut right through. Discard the stone.

3. Mash the plantain and mix in the cream cheese.

4. Stuff each date with some of the mix and gently squeeze the date back to almost its original shape.

Tip - top with a walnut piece or crushed pistachio nuts

Patti Gyapomaa Sloley

Sweet plantain & banana fritters

Plantain gives them a distinct and very different flavour to a typical banana fritter.

Makes about 10 fritters

2 plantains - over-ripe - black skin
1 banana - over-ripe - yellow with
black spots
150g/5oz rice flour
1 tsp vanilla extract
⅓ tsp mixed spice
½ tsp nutmeg, grated

oil for deep frying

1. Peel the plantain and banana, place in a bowl and mash together with a fork, then mix in the other ingredients.

2. Heat the oil in a deep pan and fry egg-size scoops in batches until golden, flipping over half way through. Remove and drain on kitchen paper.

3. Dust with a mix of cinnamon and icing sugar and serve.

Tip - add a few rays of sunshine

99

Kofi Brokeman meets a snowman

Off the grill and into a chill! Warm plantain with ice cream? I'm puckering up already!! This is scrummy all year round so don't wait for Christmas.

Definitely a fun dessert to decorate, but you'll have to hurry or the snowman will disappear before Kofi Brokeman's very eyes!! Meet him on page 19.

Serves 3

1 plantain - ripe - yellow-black skin
scoops of vanilla ice cream

Decoration suggestions:
dried fig slices
chocolate sticks
candied fruit
chocolate pieces
sprinkles
sauces
fruit coulis

Preheat the grill.

1. Peel the plantain and slice into 3 flat strips lengthways.

2. Grill under a medium heat for about 6 minutes on each side or until golden and cooked through.

3. Remove from the grill and on a board, curve each slice to form a ring, securing the ends with a cocktail stick. Don't worry if the ends don't quite meet.

Transfer into shallow serving bowls and fill each ring with a double scoop of your favourite ice cream.

Tip - put the decorations in the centre of the table and invite your friends to get artistic

101

Plum & plantain crumble

Serves 4

1 plantain - ripe - yellow-black skin
3 plums

Crumble topping:
50g/2oz porridge oats
25g/1oz caster sugar
25g/1oz ground almonds
100g/3½oz unsalted butter
75g/3oz plain flour
½ tsp cinnamon
½ tsp citrus zest
½ tsp mixed spice

Preheat oven to 200°C/fan 180°C/390°F/gas 6.

1. Peel and chop the plantain, stone and chop the plums and divide between 4 oven-proof pudding dishes.

2. Mix the crumble ingredients together, using your fingertips to form pea-size crumbs. (Or use a food processor).

3. Sprinkle the topping over the crumble base, do not press it down, and bake for 25-30 minutes until golden.

Serve with cream, custard or natural yoghurt.

Plantain chocolate truffles

This simple treat is based on a recipe from my book A Plate in the Sun. Changing the coatings brings different tastes.

Makes about 16 truffles

1 plantain - ripe - yellow-black skin
50g/2oz dried fruit mix, finely chopped
50g/2oz unsalted roasted peanuts, finely chopped

Coatings:
black and white sesame seeds
pistachio nuts, crushed
desiccated coconut

Chocolate Sauce:
115ml /4floz double cream
115g /4oz dark chocolate
Drop of vanilla extract

1. Cut off and discard the plantain ends. Slice in half crossways and then lengthways. Discard the skin. Steam for 5-8 minutes. Remove the seeds and discard.

2. Place the plantain in a bowl, mash with a fork, mix in the dried fruit and nuts then refrigerate for 30 minutes.

3. Form into 16 truffle-size balls by rolling between your palms.

4. Roll each of the balls in one of the coatings, then chill in the fridge.

5. Heat a small saucepan and add the cream. Once the cream is hot (just below boiling) remove from the heat and stir in the chocolate and vanilla. Whisk together until smooth and glossy.

6. Drizzle the sauce over the plantain truffles. Chill in the fridge before serving.

Tip - top with brightly coloured fruits, like a goji berry, coconut shaving or chopped nut

Sweet tatale

Tatale is normally a savoury pancake but it enjoys a sweet make-over with coconut and spices.

Serves 4

2 plantains - over-ripe - black skin
100g/3½oz plain flour
1 tbsp desiccated coconut
½ tsp mixed spice
25g/1oz raisins
½ tsp grated nutmeg
½ tsp ground cinnamon

oil to shallow fry

1. Peel the plantain and mash the flesh in a bowl.

2. Sift in the flour and add the remaining ingredients, mixing to form a batter. The batter should be the consistency of a scotch pancake mix. You can add a little water if you find it too thick.

3. Heat a large pan, brush it very lightly with just enough oil to stop the mix sticking then pour half-cups of the batter into the pan to form individual pancakes.

4. Cook over a moderate heat until bubbles appear then turn over and flatten with a palette knife. Fry for another minute or two until cooked through. Keep warm whilst you cook the remaining mix.

Serve with chopped fresh fruit and honey or a spicy drizzle (page 121). Scatter with toasted desiccated coconut.

Tropical chocolate fondue

Fondues are always great fun with minimum effort. Here are my tropical favourites and of course plantain is the centre piece.

Serves 4-6

Chocolate Sauce:
150ml/5floz double cream
350g /12oz dark chocolate (70%),
broken

Ideas for dipping:
1 plantain - ripe - yellow skin,
prepared as kelewele (page 23)
with which ever flavour you
prefer
chunks of: pineapple, mango, pear,
fig
whole: prunes, dates, cherries
marshmallows

Sprinkle ingredients:
gari, toasted desiccated coconut,
flaked almonds, toasted sesame
seeds

Gari is toasted cassava grains and
found in some supermarkets,
Afro-Caribbean and Asian food
shops

1. Arrange the dipping items on large plates.

2. Arrange the nuts and sprinkles on side plates.

3. Warm the cream taking care not to boil. Remove from the heat, add the chocolate and stir until completely melted. Pour into a bowl ready for dipping.

Using kebab sticks or fondue forks, skewer a piece of fruit and dip into the warm chocolate sauce then roll in the sprinkles.

...or... add meringue and make a mess...

Patti's mince tarts

A fun alternative to traditional mince pies.

Makes 4 tarts

1 plantain - ripe - yellow-black skin
1 sheet shortcrust pastry, shop
bought
4 tbsp mincemeat
1 egg, beaten

Preheat oven to 200°C/fan 180°C/390°F/gas 6.

1. Peel then slice the plantain into 4 pieces crosswise to make 4 equal cylinders.

2. Stand the plantain pieces upright on a chopping board and use an apple corer to hollow out the centres.

3. Lay the pastry flat on a floured surface and cut out 4 circles about 8 cm (3 inch) in diameter.

4. Sit the plantain pieces upright on the centre of each circle of pastry. Fill the hollow centres with mincemeat pushing it in with the end of a teaspoon.

5. Brush the pastry edges with the egg, gather up the sides and pinch together to hug the plantain.

6. Cut the remaining pastry into strips or shapes, lay across the top and brush with the egg.

7. Bake in the oven for 20-25 minutes or until the plantain and pastry are cooked and golden.

Serve with a sprinkling of icing sugar or as little islands in a sea of custard.

Tip - I bake the plantain cores at the same time as the tarts and have them as a cook's treat, sometimes rolled in gari, (toasted cassava grains)

111

Plantain & banana tart

This is based on a banana tart recipe from Mauritius. The combination of plantain and banana brings a natural sweetness. It looks a bit like a treacle tart, but with a lot less sugar, so why not?

Serves 4

1 plantain - over-ripe - black skin
1 banana - over-ripe - yellow with black spots
50g/2oz caster sugar
1 tsp vanilla extract
1 tsp coffee granules
zest of 1 orange
1 pack shop bought shortcrust pastry
1 egg yolk, beaten

Preheat oven to 180°C/fan 160°C/350°F/gas 4

1. Peel the plantain and banana and mash together with the sugar in a saucepan.

2. Place on a medium heat, stirring continuously. After 10 minutes add the remaining ingredients, except the pastry and egg, and continue to stir for 5 more minutes, or until the mixture thickens, then remove from the heat.

3. Roll the pastry to about ½ cm (¼ inch) thick and use it to line a 23 cm (9 inch) tart tin, pressing the pastry gently into the corners. Prick all over to prevent the pastry from shrinking.

4. Line the pastry with parchment paper, fill with baking beans and bake blind for 15 minutes.

5. Remove from the oven, remove the beans and parchment and fill with the plantain and banana mix.

6. Cut leftover pastry into strips to form a lattice over the tart. Brush with egg wash and bake in the oven for 25-30 minutes.

Figgie tray bake

I stumbled on this quite by accident. I had wanted to bake a plantain pudding, but my loaf tin was in the washer and I had run out of baking powder. The end result was described to me as a luscious, soft chewy-bar. I can't be sure because I think a couple of six foot mice got to it before it cooled.

Serves 4

2 plantains - over-ripe - black skin
115g/4oz sultanas
4 dried figs, roughly chopped
1 tsp mixed spice
½ tsp grated nutmeg
1 tsp vanilla extract
2 tbsp rapeseed oil
150g/5oz plain flour
4 fresh figs, quartered

Preheat oven to 180°C/fan 160°C/350°F/gas 4

1. Peel then mash the plantain in a bowl. Mix in the sultanas, dried figs, mixed spice, nutmeg, vanilla extract and rapeseed oil.

2. Sieve in the flour and gently mix again.

3. Pour into a 23cm (9 inch) square greased baking tin and place the fresh figs randomly over the top, skin side down. Bake for about 35-40 minutes. Guard carefully whilst it cools.

Plantain, date & raspberry smoothie

I love making my own smoothies, it's quick and simple and you know exactly what's in them. This is a raw plantain smoothie! Yes, raw plantain!

Serves 2

1 plantain - over-ripe - black skin
100g/3½oz frozen raspberries
2 medjool dates, stone removed
water, to thin out

1. Peel the plantain and place in a blender.

2. Add the raspberries, dates and up to 50 ml water and blend to a puree. If necessary thin with a little more water.

Serve in a glass and garnish with chopped dates.

Tip - just about any type of fresh, frozen or dried fruit will work well. A drop of vanilla extract or a teaspoon of honey makes a pleasant change

Tip - a combination of dates and green vegetable, like baby spinach or broccoli, provide a surprising flavour

117

Galliano, plantain & passionfruit griddle

A banana liqueur and sweet ripe plantain. Is this a match made in heaven?

Serves 4

4 ripe passion fruit
2 tbsp Galliano
250g/9oz mascarpone
2 tbsp icing sugar
¼ tsp vanilla extract
4 tbsp runny honey
2 plantains - ripe - yellow skin
(keep the skin on)

1. Scoop the passion fruit flesh and seeds into a bowl, mix in 1 tablespoon of Galliano and set aside.

2. Put the mascarpone, icing sugar and vanilla in a bowl, mix with a fork, cover and chill.

3. Mix the honey and remaining Galliano in a small bowl.

4. Cut the plantain in half lengthwise with the skins still on. With the tip of a knife score the flesh with deep criss-cross slashes, taking care not to go all the way through and not to cut the skin.

5. Brush the cut sides of the plantain with about half of the honey mix and grill for 4-5 minutes on a medium heat, basting occasionally with the remaining honey mix until cooked through and golden. Thick plantain may take a little longer to cook.

Serve in their skins with the mascarpone or a scoop of ice cream and drizzled with the passion fruit mix.

Poached plantain in spicy drizzle

Aromatic and fragrant. I love the winning combination of spices used by Jean-Christophe Novelli in his fabulous tarte tatin and after 3 years working at his Academy I'm hooked... Here I poach plantain in a spice syrup until they are soft and candied and serve with exotic fruits.

Serves 4

½ plantain - ripe - yellow skin

Syrup ingredients:
200ml/7floz water
115g/4oz caster sugar
½ vanilla bean, sliced in half
lengthways
2 star anise
4 green cardamom pods
2 pieces liquorice root
1 cinnamon stick
2cm/1 inch root ginger, peeled,
thinly sliced

fresh fruits:
1 pineapple
1 papaya
1 ripe mango

Tip - delicious served over ice
cream or natural yoghurt

1. Peel, then chop the plantain into ½ cm (¼ inch) discs.

2. Put the syrup ingredients in a pan and bring to a boil. Once the sugar dissolves add the plantain and simmer until syrupy, allowing the plantain to poach and cook through.

3. Remove from the heat and leave to cool then chill in the fridge, preferably overnight.

4. Peel, core, de-seed and slice the fresh fruits and put in a shallow bowl. Drizzle with the plantain spicy syrup and serve.

Plantain berry muffins

What better than a warm, freshly baked muffin with your coffee?

Makes 8 muffins

1 plantain - ripe - yellow-black skin
1 tsp vanilla extract
4 eggs
90g/3oz butter, softened
90g/3oz golden caster sugar
175g/6oz self-raising flour
90g/3oz apple sauce
zest of 1 orange
assorted berries, about 6 for each muffin

Preheat oven to 200°C/fan 180°C/390°F/gas 6.

1. Line 8 holes of a deep muffin tin with muffin cases.

2. Peel the plantain, dice and set aside.

3. Add the vanilla to the eggs and beat together.

4. Beat the butter and sugar in a mixing bowl until pale and fluffy.

5. Add some of the eggs and a tablespoon of the flour and beat. Repeat until all the eggs and flour are added.

6. Gently fold in the apple sauce, most of the plantain pieces and berries, the orange zest and remaining flour, taking care not to over mix. Reserve some of the plantain and berries for a topping.

7. Spoon the mix equally into the muffin cases.

8. Top with remaining berries and plantain pieces.

9. Bake for 30 minutes, until the muffins are risen and golden and until a skewer inserted comes out clean.

Allow to cool on a wire rack. Best eaten warm.

Patti's plantain tapas

This is an exciting way to introduce plantain and enjoy its versatility. For a sunny afternoon or evening get together, some of these recipes are perfect for a tapas-style party and can be prepared in advance. Simply add *your* favourite toppings.

Did you know?

Plantain comes in many varieties, shapes and sizes. From the small, smooth-skinned East African matoke, to the slender West African apim, to the larger, more angular varieties we are used to seeing in Afro-Caribbean and Asian food shops. In my recipes I use this latter variety.

Plantain is a member of the banana family, an herbaceous plant of the genus musa and the largest herb in the world.

Gluten and cholesterol free, low in sodium, high in potassium and vitamins A and B6, very high in vitamin C.

They grow all year round so there's no "Season" and, unlike bananas, their ripening doesn't need to be artificially managed.

Native to India, and spread around the world by traders, they now grow in most tropical climates.

Although it's often called the cooking cousin of the banana I've recently discovered it can be eaten raw.

Similar to its fruity cousin the banana, it's often used like a vegetable. More starchy and lower in sugar than bananas, it is sometimes thought of as the tropical equivalent of pasta or potato.

Sweet recipes using over-ripe plantain often don't need refined sugar.

Fermented plantain is used to make beer in East Africa.

Green plantain porridge is popular in parts of Africa and the West Indies.

Plantain leaves can be used as wraps to bake in and a plate to serve on.

Probably one of the most popular uses of green plantain in Ghana is to boil it, then pound it into large, dough-like dumplings called fufu and serve with ladles of delicious soup. Although traditionally it's pounded with a 5 foot long wooden pestle and matching mortar, thankfully you can now buy packets of instant fufu.

On the left - Matoke

In the centre - Apim

On the right - larger varieties as I use in my recipes

Cook's Notes

Scotch bonnet chillies can be pierced then put in whole to release their flavour and control the amount of heat. I taste the food regularly as it cooks and remove the pepper when the heat is right.

I occasionally refer to a sliver of scotch bonnet because chilli heat is a matter of taste. The bigger the sliver the hotter the dish. I love scotch bonnets for their fruity flavour and heat although other hot peppers and powdered varieties like cayenne work equally well.

Fresh herbs are always my first choice, but if you use dried herbs reduce the quantities accordingly as they are more intense.

Freshly ground black peppercorns are my first choice anywhere I mention pepper for seasoning.

Cookers vary in performance, you may need to adjust cooking times to suit the appliance you are using.

Use your own judgement to decide when food is properly cooked.

All eggs in the recipes are large and free range unless otherwise stated.

All vegetable, herbs and fruits should be washed before use.

Use your own judgement to decide if fruits and vegetables should be peeled.

Conversions from metric to imperial measures are not exact, but will not affect the recipes.

My favourite oils for cooking are: rapeseed, groundnut, palm fruit and olive. The palm fruit oil and rapeseed blend I use is available in many supermarkets and is from certified sustainable sources.

My favourite rice is basmati.

Before I start cooking I like to assemble and prepare all of the ingredients, it makes it so much quicker, easier and more fun.

My ingredients can usually be found in supermarkets, Afro-Caribbean and Asian food shops, and of course the internet.

I find using heavy based pans makes cooking easier as the heat is more evenly distributed.

All of the food photographed in this book was cooked by Patti and eaten and enjoyed by family and friends.

Six-foot mice- so that's where all the food disappeared!

Fun days at the Academy

As front-of-house and a resident chef at the Novelli Academy how lucky am I to be working with Jean-Christophe, so many top chefs and a fabulous and friendly support team.

I enjoy good food and meeting new people (my husband translates that to eating and talking, he may have a point there).

Courses are run in Jean-Christophe's charming farmhouse family kitchen. I arrive to the aroma of stocks simmering, biscuits baking and good coffee, and the kitchen buzzing in preparation for the day.

The excitement starts with the arrival, meeting and greeting of the guests, then we settle in for expert guidance and spoonfuls of food heaven.

The day is punctuated with fun and laughter, there's never a dull moment!

Acknowledgements - Mi daase pii

Mum, what can I say? Our home always has a warm and welcoming table of eagerly awaited treats for family and friends. Without your wonderful cooking and influence I wouldn't have done any of this.

Jeff, for supporting, encouraging and believing in me. The amount of work that has gone into producing this book – from photography right through to publication, all whilst holding down a full-time job! Your patience every time I changed my mind. (and it was frequently!). It would have been impossible without you.

Ed and Dave, for your technical support and for testing and enjoying my cooking, even though you sometimes ate the exhibits before we had chance to photograph them!!

Jean-Christophe and Michelle, for having confidence in me, allowing me to develop my passion and supporting and encouraging me whole-heartedly.

The entire Novelli Team for your encouragement. A special thanks to Felice - how many times did you let me talk about my passion for plantain during your courses, earning me the name 'Plantain Patti'. Viva Ghana and Italy!

Family and friends, for tasting and loving my food and all your beautiful comments.

All the people I haven't even met, yet have made such positive comments. You give me the confidence to continue exploring and sharing.

I feel very lucky indeed. Thank you all from the bottom of my heart.

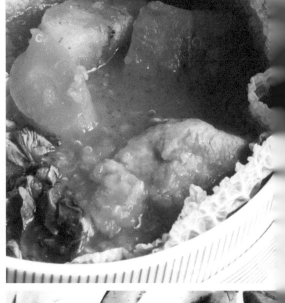

Adinkra

The symbols in this book are from Patti's book - Ghana's Adinkra: Symbols from our African Heritage

Bi Nka Bi
"No one should hurt another" - peace, harmony, kinship, fair play

Nyame Dua
"Tree of god" or "Holy place" - God's protection and presence

Nyame Nnwu Na Mawu
"God never dies, therefore I cannot die" - life after death, God's omnipresence and eternal existence

Ananse Ntontan
"Spider's web" - wisdom, creativity, craftiness, good judgement

Mpatapo
"Knot of reconciliation" - peace-making, reconciliation, agreement, coming together

Sankofa
"San ko fa" - Go back and get it, learn from the past.

Gye Nyame
"Except God" - the omnipotence, omnipresence and supremacy of God.

Akoma Ntoso
"Linked hearts" - understanding, agreement, unity, harmony

Ese Ne Tekrema
"The teeth and the tongue" - friendship, harmony, interconnection, interdependence

Nyame Biribi Wo Soro
"God is in the heavens" hope, belief in God

Odo Nyera Fie Kwan
"Love will always find its way home" - the power of love and devotion

Akoma
"The heart" - patience, tolerance, compassion

Sankofa
"San ko fa" - Go back and get it, learn from the past.

More about Adinkra:
The Adinkra Dictionary: A Visual Primer on the Language of Adinkra by W Bruce Willis, published by The Pyramid Complex, ISBN: 0-9661532-0-0
www.Adinkra.org   (Includes a bibliography from "The Adinkra Dictionary")

Right: Plantain grove, Dixcove Hill, Takoradi, Ghana